A MENNONITE WOMAN'S LIFE

A MENNONITE WOMAN'S LIFE

Ruth Hershey, 1895-1990
Photographer

Phyllis Pellman Good
Author

Photographs selected and printed by Edwin P. Huddle
(a grandson of Ruth Hershey)

Good Books

Intercourse, PA 17534

Design by Dawn J. Ranck

Library of Congress Cataloging-in-Publication Data

To all Mennonite farm women who,
through their own powerful ingenuity,
endured the demands on their lives.

"Home was, without question,
the center of the Mennonite world.
It was there that babies were born,
young people were married,
and grandparents lived
out their retirement years."

Table of Contents

Ruth Hershey,
Mennonite Farm Woman
and Photographer

She must have been, or so it seems now, a quiet radical. Her simple hairstyle and clothing choices did not betray the splendid strength of her creative eye. Nor was she pushed to the margins of her highly disciplined church community for her nonconforming pleasures.

Ruth Hershey, modest Mennonite woman, came to maturity during the Depression, joined the church, married, farmed, and built a family. Yet she never laid aside her box camera. Instead, she routinely disappeared into a wedge of a closet under the front steps in the hallway to develop her own film in complete darkness, while her children flowed through the rest of the farmhouse. (All that before electricity came to the Hershey farm, just outside Paradise, Pennsylvania, in eastern Lancaster County.)

Ruth Hershey was made of sturdy material. Her parents

were first cousins, and Ruth credited that genetic wallop for her strong will. "Children may inherit double a character trait," she explained about herself. And, in fact, she needed that reservoir of strength. Life did not begin gently for this first child of John and Maze Hershey.

In 1898, when Ruth was two-and-a-half years old, and her brother John was a three-month old infant, their mother was nipped by a train at the Leaman Place Crossing, just outside Paradise, and lost her lower right leg. Maze saw a child crossing the main line railroad track, as was customary, but this time in the path of an oncoming train. She pushed him out of the way, saving his life, but when she stumbled and fell, the train ran over her leg. Maze was rushed by that same train to a hospital in Philadelphia for emergency surgery.

Thereafter Maze walked with a limp because of her prosthetic leg and was limited physically. But she bore seven more children and shared the work with eldest daughter Ruth, who saw it this way, "I had to look after the young ones because Mom couldn't."

She grew up quickly, assertively, capably. Custom and her mother's injury kept Ruth from completing high school. But neither of those matters prevented her discovery of other worlds. She became a voracious reader, especially novels by

Ruth Hershey at home with her camera. "She was the first person I knew who had a camera," observes her sister-in-law Alice Hershey, born two years before Ruth and still alert at 100 years of age.

Marietta Holley. The heroes were women, cast as persons of influence, with men as mere appendages. It was literature that reflected the mood of the day—women's suffrage and the temperance movement. Ruth Hershey couldn't stop reading. But if Holley's stories entranced her, they didn't draw her away from the Mennonite church community. Instead, she found quietly acceptable diversions.

She learned to play the organ. She amassed piles of sheet music.

She drove a "machine" early in her life. Because of Maze's handicap, John bought a car ahead of many of his fellow church members. (He also installed a bathroom and running water in the kitchen before most of his neighbors, again for the convenience of his wife.) In eastern Pennsylvania, licenses became mandatory for drivers in 1914. Ruth's was issued that year. She was 18 years old.

But she found absolute expression in the box camera that came her way during her mid-teens. She experimented. She documented. She spontaneously recorded what she loved most.

In a world where teenagers were expected to work hard and young women were prepared to marry, equipped with serving, cooking, gardening, housekeeping, and childrearing skills—all in an attitude of quiet faithfulness to one's spouse and church—Ruth Hershey had a few extra resources. She proved able to skirt the Mennonite community's tendency to make work a sacrament and the pleasure of creative expression suspicious, if not sinful.

She was no slacker—there was never time for that! But neither was she a slave to the crowd of responsibilities that overlapped her life.

Ruth Hershey worked at home for her parents until she was 21. Ever a learner and lover of people, she then took up practical nursing, training herself from books that advocated home nursing and with the guidance of local doctors. She packed her two-year career with numerous cases, assisting with the births of 17 babies one year.

When Ruth Hershey fell in love, it was with Willis Hershey from down the road. Woman of strength married man of meekness. They discovered each other at the Paradise Mennonite Sunday school where she attended with her family and he came with the neighbors. Willis' parents belonged to the Old Order group that didn't have Sunday school. Maze and John were part of the more progressive church. That difference didn't derail Willis' and Ruth's romance, although Ruth wasn't sure her sisters-in-law approved of her special pleasures. And her mother-in-law asked that she please not take her picture. Ruth could live with that.

When Ruth and Willis married in 1918, they set up housekeeping in Ruth's family homestead. That was a bit out of the ordinary since farms usually passed to a son. But Ruth's brothers weren't ready to assume farming responsibilities, and she was the oldest of eight, and the only daughter who married. So she and Willis began buying the farm, and the elder Hersheys and their at-home brood moved to nearby Cherry Hill.

The children began arriving soon thereafter—Marian in 1919; Mildred in 1922; Dorothy in 1924; Katherine in 1927; J. Robert in 1931; Ruth Naomi in 1933; Hulda in 1936.

The Depression threaded through the Lancaster County farmland, and Ruth and Willis Hershey felt it keenly. But they only grew more resourceful as they worked to make farm payments, and to shelter, feed, and clothe their youngsters.

Ruth turned to making cup cheese, a stringy spread made with sour milk. When the local milk company cut out their pickup of milk one day each week, she refused to pour the milk away. Instead, she found a market for cup cheese in some nearby factories and broadened the family's income. Soon her children were carrying along her homemade potato chips and doughnuts, offering them for sale as well. And in the spring, the family peddled Ruth's asparagus, sugar peas, and strawberries.

She planted a garden and a truck patch, she stored up food for the winter, she cleaned the gargantuan farmhouse, she fashioned children's clothing out of cotton feedbags—and through it all she kept her camera at hand.

Never physically strong, this woman of emotional power and certainty knew how not to be buried by work and worry. Although work was ever present, she learned not to be its slave. She had found too much satisfaction in reading, in music, and in photography, and she carried raw reminders of life's brevity. She gave birth to a stillborn child in 1926. She lost three-month-old Ruth in 1934 to kidney failure. Her sister Rhoda died in 1925 at the age of 24. And Maze was gone in 1935, victim of a car accident. Ruth, it seemed, managed a life-giving balance within herself, through it all.

There were trade-offs, to be sure! When Ruth worked in her sliver of a darkroom, she couldn't be cleaning. And when she took her daily afternoon nap, she wasn't baking. She didn't sew and read at the same time. But she made choices that preserved her spirit and happiness and that created a home where resourceful children grew.

Youngest daughter Hulda guesses that "ninety percent of the people in our community didn't know what all Mother could

Ruth (left) and her sister Rhoda. Remarks Alice Hershey, her friend and peer, "Ruth wasn't afraid to try things. She wasn't afraid to step out. But she wasn't on the fringe; she was a leader. And she was a great saver. I'm so glad she saved her negatives."

do!" If her diversions were a secret to all but her family, the surrounding Mennonite world may have noticed a few wrinkled edges in her homemaking. "Things were liveable," recalls Hulda, "but not necessarily tip-top! The house wasn't always totally clean and the grass around the walks not perfectly trimmed. But she didn't neglect her family."

What one's children remember of home may be incomplete, but what they recall of its attitude and atmosphere is likely to be full of much truth. Ruth Hershey's children tell a consistent story. They do it, of course, in a properly Mennonite fashion: by first reflecting humbly on themselves! Dorothy explains, "We're all good housekeepers. We're not sloppy, but we have other things we like to do! Mother was a good housekeeper, too. But she had meticulous relatives who all they did was clean. She did things she enjoyed.

"She made sure we had other interests and that we all went to high school. She wanted us all to be prepared to do something beyond housework."

Ruth Hershey opened the windows for all her children. Remarkably, she did it without spinning them out of the Mennonite church which was, at the same time, becoming increasingly explicit about appropriate behavior for its members.

"She owned a complete set of Dickens," Marian remembers.

"Later, a couple we met in Ocean City gave her a whole set of Shakespeare. I don't know if she read them all, but she liked having the books.

"At bedtime we would often be in her bed while she read to us. When she and Dad went to the Sesquicentennial in Philadelphia, they brought us each a book."

Mildred remembers that "Mother allowed us to be in plays and operettas and cantatas. She didn't mind if we learned the dance steps. In fact, she even made me a skirt for that. She wasn't a strict person in that way!"

Ruth Hershey never lived an open rebellion. Neither did she practice one set of standards publicly and a different one back the lane in Paradise. She simply understood the church's concern for disciplined living and attempted to follow its direction without denying the curiosity and zest to experiment that moved within her.

"Mother and Daddy were always careful to explain that the church looked out for our good," Katherine recalls. "'You may not understand that now,' they would say. 'They're not trying to be mean. You may understand more later.' And then, because we had no church youth groups, they allowed us to be part of Rural Youth, a large secular organization that sponsored all kinds of social activities."

That love of the church—yet interest in much of life beyond

its borders—continued to characterize Ruth Hershey's choices.

"She always got magazines. When I was in high school, she subscribed to *Saturday Evening Post, Good Housekeeping,* and all the church papers," Mildred explains. "She bought a large dictionary that had all kinds of math and science tables in the back. It was probably expensive, but a good investment. I used it a lot!"

Dorothy remembers the mushroom experiment. "She'd see something and she'd think, 'I can do that'—like growing mushrooms. She got horse manure to get these little plants started out in the back corner of a shed. I can't recall if we ever had any to use, but I do remember her going out with a lantern—we didn't have electricity—to check them!"

"She had piles of sheet music. I remember," says Mildred, "when we got a piano, and she said, 'Now I can play the octaves the way the piece is written.' Until then she had played on a pump organ with a shorter keyboard. She had a beautiful touch.

"Our parents didn't pray aloud, but we often sang a lot of hymns after supper. Mother would go in and play the organ, and Daddy would join us to sing before he went out to finish up the work. All of us six children were given piano lessons and lessons on another instrument of our choice."

Not all was harmonious, however. Ruth and Willis, drawn to each other by their complementary strengths, tangled at times. And Ruth's children were, on occasion, certain that she was kinder to the neighbors and tramps who came to the door than she was to her own daughters and son! "'I just didn't want to spoil my children,' she said to us later. 'Maybe I *was* a little too hard on you.'"

It is the confession of a woman of strength and principle.

Ruth Hershey was almost bigger than her world. Those who knew her most intimately bear many benefits and some scars from that. "It was hard for her to admit she was wrong. It was hard for any of us children to outdo her. At times Mother tried to make some of our decisions for us. Later she learned to accept our choices, even if it was hard for her," remarks Hulda.

Yet Ruth kept finding ways to enlarge her world when it threatened to close in on her. In the late 1930s, she began hosting visitors to Lancaster County. No major commercial effort would be made to draw tourists to the area for another twenty years, but Ruth learned of some travelers looking for a place to stay. "I was seven or eight at the time," Robert reflects. "We had extra space by then, and she liked it to be used. That was good stewardship! She liked cooking and visiting, and I'm sure that instigated the idea. Economics would have been secondary."

Once again, Ruth Hershey found a way to thrive in her relatively confined setting. Hosting tourists consumed her energy for years. "She didn't stay within the Mennonite community for her friendships," remarks Hulda who was growing up during the years that tourists peopled the house. Ruth soon learned to set boundaries for her guests. "Many stayed for a week or two," says Katherine who was eleven when the first group arrived. "Mother would cook full meals for them. One week we had fifteen—a bunch of undisciplined city kids." Even Ruth Hershey had her limits. "Mother said, 'Never again!'" She took fewer visitors at a time from then on, but she continued hosting tourists until 1977 when she was nearly eighty-two. Late that year, Willis fell ill and died a few months later in early 1978.

Soon thereafter she moved in with her daughter Mildred; then went on to the Mennonite Home where she lived for nearly eleven years.

She had given up photography in those later years and turned, instead to making quilts and comfort tops, still finding satisfaction in exploring the world visually.

Ruth Hershey died in 1990. But her legacy of life through photographs continues.

A Wife

Marriage among Mennonites was serious business. Most members married within the church. Men and women selected their own mates, but the church community lent its weight to keeping marriages together. If difficulty developed, most couples found it less troublesome to stay together than to leave the marriage and risk the disapproval of church and family alike.

Farm life meant that husbands and wives ate three meals together nearly every day, and that they saw each other throughout the day, sometimes working outdoors together; at other times conferring about decisions and tasks. A sort of partnership developed between some couples, although within the community, status was clear—the men were primarily responsible; the women were considered "helpmeet."

Traditionally, Mennonites have been a reserved people, particularly reticent about their deepest feelings. Husbands and wives seldom expressed their affection for each other

Willis and Ruth Hershey married in 1918. Together
they farmed, reared six children to adulthood, lived
faithfully within the Mennonite church, struggled
with their different personal styles, and sang.

openly. They were expected, however, to show each other respect. Usually there were children nearby, and their instruction, both directly and indirectly, was the responsibility of their parents. How to treat, and behave as, a spouse was top agenda in this society where marriage and family were foundational matters.

Being a wife was a responsibility demanding skills. And training started early. Young girls were taught to clean, do basic kitchen chores, and help with laundry. More difficult jobs followed—caring for children, sewing one's own clothes, baking bread and pies, picking vegetables in the garden, working in the yard.

Most often, training came gently and continually at the elbow of one's mother or alongside one's grandmother or aunts. Now and then, epidemics and accidents sprang young women into heavy responsibility, too early and too quickly.

A married woman's life in the traditional Mennonite community of the early 1900s was measured by the quality of all she was responsible for—the character of her children; the cleanliness and upkeep of her house, yard, flowerbeds, and gardens; her ability to cook, sew, and be a hostess; and those more ambiguous areas, such as how well she managed, what all she accomplished, and whether her husband was known as a person of respect and integrity.

A Mother

One may have trained as a teacher or been active as a nurse, but one's greatest wish as a Mennonite woman in the early decades of this century was to be a mother.

If all was well, health-wise, babies came fast and continually after marriage. There was usually no good reason, short of illness or poverty, to worry about birth control. In rural settings and especially on farms, a sizeable family was a helpful work force. Among Mennonites, children were viewed as gifts and blessings from God, as well as much needed labor for the heavy tasks at hand.

Next to one's faith and the church, family was highly treasured. Among Mennonites it was almost assumed, like good soil and fresh air, because it was so constant and so present. Yet Sunday sermons and wedding meditations and the intense interest the church took in holding husbands, wives, and children together in harmony, all revealed the community's high regard for family.

A sense of tribe was celebrated and cultivated. In this part of the country, children frequently received their mother's maiden

← The Hersheys at home, about 1933. Willis and Ruth with their children (left to right) Marian (born 1919), Mildred (born 1922), Dorothy (born 1924), Katherine (born 1927), and Robert (born 1931).

↑ The Hershey farmstead sprawled on fertile ground in eastern Lancaster County. It was Ruth's family home. Eventually Willis' parents retired in three first-floor rooms in the brick (left) end of the house.

A spread of daffodils covered the hillside across the
stream that ran through the farm.

name as their middle name. It was not unusual for all the siblings in a family to have that same middle name.

Making genealogical connections was an entrancing game and filled hours of visiting for those middle-aged and older. It was a community-sustaining, *freundschaft*-building exercise. Not only was one thus placed genealogically; one seldom escaped being ascribed commonly perceived distinguishing family characteristics!

Extended family often defined one's social sphere (supplemented, of course, by one's church friends and sometimes one's neighbors). Grandparents, aunts and uncles, in-laws, and cousins gathered to share farm work and gardening, to relax and visit, to prepare for weddings and plan funerals.

Here one found one's identity, developed kinship glue, learned appropriate behavior, and experienced a nest of belonging. This was one's fortress against a sometimes inhospitable surrounding society.

Pastoral and peaceful as it may appear, brothers and sisters competed for their parents' affection, sometimes received imbalanced inheritances, and took more or less an equal share in caring for their aging parents. Now and then family amplified trouble. But more often, family fended off difficulty and preserved its members from loneliness.

Robert and Hulda (born 1936) with some of the
animals that filled the home place, about 1941. The
steam engine in the background was stored on the
Hershey farm and used in mid-summer by the
threshing gang of which Willis was a part.

Robert Hershey, the only son of Ruth and Willis, became a polio victim in his early teens. He was hospitalized for nine weeks, and Ruth went in to care for him daily. During that time, Ruth's father died. Adding to their grief was Robert's disappointment that he couldn't attend his grandfather's funeral. Robert and Grandfather John had grown quite close, and Robert was beginning to show interest in taking over the farm, which had earlier belonged to the older man.

Robert's health prevented him from farming. Eventually he was ordained as a minister in the Mennonite church.

Work

Work was a full-bodied figure in the Mennonite farm world. It filled the landscape, the house, the barn. It wrapped around and through life, both demanding and giving. While it consumed hours and lifeblood, it also conferred meaning and held families close to each other.

Mennonites raised their children to meet work head on, never to avoid it, not even to quarrel with it. That doesn't mean they always enjoyed it. But in spite of that, they learned to work. By example.

For the most part, tradition and training determined who worked where. Women managed the house, the yard, the small garden, the cooking, and the sewing. Men supervised the barn, fields, and livestock. There were those areas that each couple had to negotiate—care of the large garden, discipline of the children, major family purchases.

If one worked constantly, it was seldom alone. Many children and extended family lifted the burden higher, and sometimes the neighbors helped.

Imagine a farm woman's life without electricity. Instead of a refrigerator, she kept food cold on the floor and along the walls of the spring house. She carried the family laundry to the wash house, usually attached to the farm house kitchen. There she washed clothing in water heated in enormous iron or copper kettles set over a two-hole furnace, fueled by wood and chips stored in the woodshed. Cooking happened on the cookstove, powered by coal or wood.

In contrast to many of her friends, Ruth Hershey had running water in her kitchen before electricity. The water drained by gravity from a tank in an upstairs room. Drinking water came from the spring through a pipeline to a pump on the porch.

When electricity arrived in the rural areas surrounding Paradise, it was the result of a community decision. When enough farmers were convinced of its value and were ready to foot the bill, electric power lines were laid through the fields. It was 1936 and the older Hershey children were half grown. But by then the Depression was in full swing, which cleared away any hope of life becoming easier now that electricity had come.

Ruth was prepared, and so were her adolescent daughters. "The Depression made her more resourceful," Mildred believes. Katherine, who enjoyed her assignment to peddle

Farming was almost always an intergenerational affair. Children too young to help were nonetheless present, deepening their sense of family and security. Husbands and wives tackled some projects together, allowing a greater sense of partnership.

35

Harvest-time and butchering usually required the
hands of more than the farmer's immediate family.
Neighbors and extended family came to help in these
seasonal events—and had their favor returned when
their crops were ready and their hogs fattened.

The most mundane work took on a tone of near-fun when adult siblings, cousins, and grandparents joined the effort. Here in the early decades of the century, part of the Hershey clan gathers corn in the early fall.

the family's fresh vegetables in town, agrees. "We kids didn't even know there was a Depression." The two sisters recall that because they could find no market for the abundance of eggs their chickens produced, their mother turned to making noodles. And she systematically mapped out the chores so everyone had responsibility, without being overcome by the merciless stream of work.

Ruth Hershey knew how to pace herself. Because the work was endless, she got ahead of it by managing. She started working before dawn, but she built in rest time for herself every day. She read the paper or listened to the radio after electricity came. In between, she disappeared into her darkroom.

She allowed her children similar breaks. "We had off Saturday afternoons. We had to have all our chores done by noon; then the rest of the day was ours," they still recall with sweet pleasure.

Ruth's ability to take charge of her work load, without being cowered by it, brought grace to her own life and her family's. "She taught us how to sew by hand, how to cook, and we had a piano teacher come to the house to give us all lessons," Dorothy remembers now in one breath.

"Daddy was part of a threshing rig. I remember making pies in the morning when they were coming to our house. Mother

Never afraid to experiment, Ruth Hershey, photographer, here attempted to capture motion on film. Hulda feeds the chickens and visits with drop-in company in the late 1940s.

Farming as teamwork—for mules, young men, and boys.

Barn raisings were community events. Men, under the direction of a job foreman, swung hammers and hoisted beams. Women, supervised by the farm wife, prepared roasters of meat, kettles of mashed potatoes and vegetables, platters of bread, and an abundance of cakes, pies, and puddings.

would work us real hard in the morning; then she'd say we could go off in the afternoon to watch. She didn't drive us constantly."

There was a certain amount of chivalry at play in this hard-working, no-nonsense society. Willis Hershey didn't ask his wife to work in the fields or the barn, except early on when she helped with the milking before the couple had a hired man. Willis also worked the truck patch, the larger of the family's two gardens, and cared for the orchard.

There was one other valve in this otherwise stalwart setting. "We always had hired girls when we were small," explained Mildred. "They came from the Millersville Children's Home [an orphanage operated by the local Mennonite churches] to help with the housework, especially the laundry." Ruth, in keeping with her particular delight in people, stayed in touch with these young women for years after they left her employ.

In contrast to many of her Mennonite peers, Ruth Hershey permitted her standards of tidiness to dip slightly so that she could find a rhythm between work and pleasure. "She managed to read a lot," recall her daughters. "And every now and then she'd say, 'Get your work done early today.' Then she'd take us on a picnic, or fishing or swimming down in the creek."

Ruth's camera recorded the nearly unbelievable!
Willis and a cohort show off their fish in the front
yard of the Hershey farm.

Friends

Visiting—or the promise of it—held ever-present work and the isolation of farm life somewhat at bay. Some farmsteads had telephones before 1940, but when Mennonite families first installed them, they were intended to be utilitarian, although party lines did supply occasional pleasure!

Throughout the week, the mail and one's family were one's only certain diversions from responsibility. And so it was that weekends brought respite from bone-wearying work, the chance for fun and fellowship, and a renewed sense of one's place in the community. "Getting together" was an institution that nourished the soul.

Some events were spontaneous, others intricately planned. Drop-in company was welcome on Saturday night. It was anticipated Sunday afternoon or evening. Extended family, church friends, and acquaintances from one's teenage years could appear without warning and be warmly received, often with bountiful food.

Ruth Hershey learned to drive a car in her mid-teens—an

← The big girls mama-ed the little girls. It was both relaxation and education; the way they learned the skills that would be expected of them later in life.

Dorothy holds Hulda on the Hershey front porch. Looking at them is their cousin Martha Hershey Kreider. Katherine holds down the rocking chair, viewed by her cousin Erma Hershey Lehman.

↑ Hulda, Martha, Katherine, and Erma.

The quintessential world of Mennonite women, about 1920. The primary themes are present—the extended family, from babies to grandmothers (Grandma Maze is in the white apron; the boy at the far left and the three girls at the right are her younger children), hospitality (the clothing indicates a weekend get-together), work (Grandma Maze appears to have been busy in the kitchen), and pleasure, derived largely from visiting.

The men visited, too, but in another part of the yard.
Cigars were a Sunday afternoon treat. On summer
days the house shutters were closed, in an effort to
keep the house cool.

Many Mennonite farm families hosted Fresh Air children for several weeks each summer. Children from nearby cities were welcomed and swept into farm life as a respite from their customary tight space and urban surroundings.

Katherine (in the middle) and Mildred (at the far right) line up with some of Grandma Maze's Fresh Air girls and extended family.

ironic advantage from her mother's accident with the train. Ever the social being, Ruth could escape her adult-sized responsibilities while still a teenager and go to singing school, girl crowd gatherings, and revival meetings. Those young women without cars could ride trolleys around Lancaster County and into the city, choosing from camp meetings or young people's meetings.

Mennonites at this time were becoming increasingly distinguished from their neighbors and surrounding communities. World War I brought their convictions of nonresistance and conscientious objection to war into public view. Their discomfort with the growing nationalism prodded them to define their differences with the prevailing society and to develop clearer guidelines for their own behavior. Distinctive dress patterns began to be prescribed. Church statements of discipline addressed whether or not members should vote or participate in labor unions. And as the differences became more sharply outlined, the faith community began to strengthen its own social connections. It began to provide for and permit more occasions for members to get together and to develop kinship.

And so it was that Ruth Hershey and her peers gathered in girl crowds, each Saturday at a different homestead, to play games, sew for their hope chests, pick wildflowers, and eat

Family and friends together.

Young women, who had not yet joined the Mennonite church, were not expected to wear distinctive plain clothing. These are some of Ruth's friends.

The daffodil hillside on the Hershey farm.

extravagantly. On other weekends they joined a family reunion, one of those meetings of a tribe bound together by well-known stories, quixotic characters, favorite foods.

Marriage and children brought shifts in a couple's social life. They joined smaller groupings; they sought out the brothers and sisters they no longer saw every day. Babies and toddlers changed the nature of such events. Mildred and Katherine remember that their mother, in the thick of her childrearing years, "often had headaches on Sundays. Sometimes we had company. Daddy would pass out cigars to all the men lined up on the porch. And Mother would serve pie and angel food cakes!"

Growing children continued to affect a family's social activities. The Hersheys' practices were common ones. "Mother and Daddy both participated in singing schools [church-sponsored lessons in a cappella sight-reading of music, usually hymns]. Then we would all sing what they had learned around the piano. Daddy's parents lived in the brick end of our house, and when their other children and grandchildren came to visit, we played our instruments—trumpet, clarinet, violin, and piano—and all sang together."

This was a world of warmth and remarkable flexibility, given its growing sense of threat from the larger world.

Friends in the fall. Ruth (fourth from left) with a
group of young women, all of whom are members of
the church, as is clear by their dress.

In the earliest decades of the twentieth century, many young Lancaster Mennonite women joined a "circle." These groups usually included about twelve women who met monthly to visit and work on projects together. Some of those circles continue to meet today. Others gradually disappeared as women grew increasingly busy with children, church and community activities, and jobs outside their homes.

Girl crowds, in contrast to circles, were larger
groupings and more fluid. Invited guests changed,
reflecting the hostess' friendships. This summertime
event included croquet.

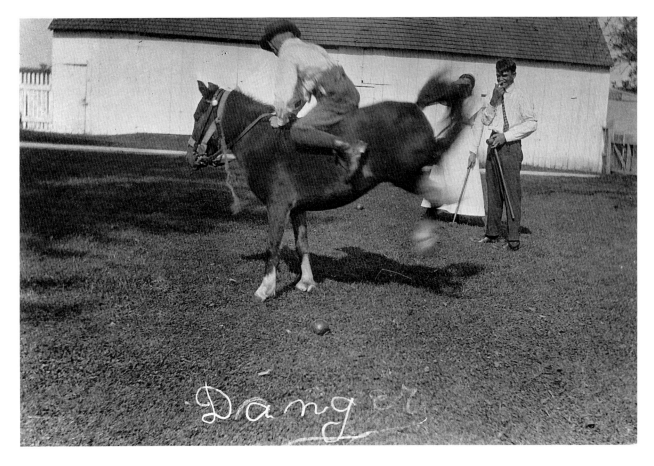

Danger

↑ Little brothers have always found ways to create some excitement at their older siblings' parties.

→ Ruth (in the center) experimented continually with angles in her composition.

They may have been plain, but Ruth Hershey (far right) and her friends were still fashion-conscious. Notice their cinched waists and watch fobs (lapped over the belts of the women second and third from the right).

Alice Hershey, who was also growing up at this time, notes that the woman on the far left is wearing a head covering, but no cape on her dress. That was an unusual departure during a period when the church was asking for more compliance from its members. A head covering signified submission on the part of women. Capes were designed to insure modesty. Both were expected to be worn consistently.

Sunday afternoon friends, finding pleasure in each other's company.

At Home—and Away

Home was, without question, the center of the Mennonite world. It was there that babies were born, young people were married, grandparents lived out their retirement years, viewings of the deceased were held. In most Mennonite families of this era, both parents worked at home. The homestead produced one's livelihood and year-round food supply. It was the site of most social occasions—family reunions for fun and fellowship; family get-togethers for work projects such as butchering and apple-butter-making; girl crowds and circles; games of quoits and croquet.

Responsibilities kept one close to home. Enticements away were minimal and transportation was limited. Instead, the luxury of open space, the presence of many siblings, the nearness of grandparents, cousins, aunts, and uncles—all filled one's sense of home and kept family members centered there.

Visitors were a welcome diversion. During the week there were peddlers and neighbors and tramps. They either joined

Part of the Hershey tribe. Grandmother Maze, caught in the middle of pie-baking by the unexpected visit of her sister Annie. Annie, the only one who is "dressed" in the picture, likely walked out to the farm from Paradise. With Maze are her daughter Rhoda and son George, remembered as an adult by his nieces for making them cry with his facial contortions!

Evident in this photograph is Ruth Hershey's interest in capturing daily life as it was, rather than taking shots that were static and posed.

The family seldom fed tramps, and only occasionally did they come into the house, but Ruth saw the character in these men's faces and bearings, and she wanted their pictures.

Marian remembers one tramp in particular, a World War I veteran. "He had lost an eye and an arm, and so Mother made a little room for him in the basement. Later when he moved into the County Home, she visited him there.

"Another tramp was a heavy drinker, and he had left his wife and children in Canada. Some time after he was gone from our place, he wrote to Mother to say he had gone back to his family—because of her exemplary living. Now she wasn't the kind to ask people if they were Christians. She simply lived what she believed."

in the work or provided a brief respite from it.

The Hershey farm was the last one along the Strasburg Railroad. So tramps jumped off the train there and set up camp in a far corner of the acreage. When the weather grew cold or damp, they checked in at the house for shelter and, occasionally, food. "We never fed many tramps," recalls oldest daughter, Marian, "but a lot slept there. Daddy always asked them to put their matches in a special place. Then he'd permit them to sleep in the barn."

The effort was not without its risks, however. Once a tramp bedded down in the barn with a bottle of liquor. He lost his bearings and fell through a hay hole from the second-floor mow to the cow stable on the ground floor. He hit his head on a stanchion and was bleeding from his ear when the family discovered the accident. "My mother did not approve of his drinking," reflects Marian, "but I remember how kindly she treated him. She called an ambulance and saw to it that he was hospitalized and cared for."

Home may have been a refuge, but sometimes the farming operation, the tumble of children, and the endless traffic of neighbors and extended family built to an unnerving din. Ruth Hershey looked for relief, as many mothers have through the generations. "If we had a new baby or if Mother had a headache, she'd stay home from Sunday morning

church. I think it was her quiet time," guesses now-grown Katherine. "Often during a two-week stretch of evening revival meetings at church, she didn't go. She was just glad the rest of us could!"

Yet, for the most part, the Hershey farm hummed. "Mother had birthday and Halloween parties for all of us," Dorothy remembers. "When I was a high school senior we held a party in our attic because it was too cold to be in the barn. Mother enjoyed it thoroughly."

The flow of Fresh Air children and visitors to Lancaster County started through the Hershey farm when Robert was a young boy. "She was a very outgoing woman," he remarks. It seemed her energy was restored as she made new friends. The overnight guests who came, intending to spend a few days, often became "almost boarders," Marian explains. They corresponded for years, once again enlarging Ruth's borders.

Farm families had few getaways. Dairy cattle required twice daily milkings. Crops needed continual tending. The maintenance of farm buildings was constant. And most farmers in the early decades of the twentieth century were not financially able to travel far with their growing brood of children.

On rare occasions, especially when there were fewer

The Hersheys had Amish neighbors.

members in the family, Ruth and Willis took the children to the ocean. Marian remembers one occasion when she was four. "A newly married couple ate at our table. We visited, and then kept in contact with them for years. Years later they sent Mother a whole set of Shakespeare."

Most excursions were limited to Sunday afternoon drives to or with old friends. In that was both comfort and diversion, close to home.

Ocean City and the friends she made there left their marks on
Ruth Hershey. Mildred and Katherine remember that she
learned to filet fish through her visits to the shore and began
buying shad when it was in season. "Sometimes she'd invite
guests for supper and we would have fish and French
fries—not a typical Mennonite menu for the early '40s!"

Animals were abundant on the farm. Yet some were pets.

Others were prized.

Town friends.

Sometimes excitement came to the farm. Other times
the young people went elsewhere to find it. Ruth, who
was driving at age 16, used her advantage to the delight
of her friends. "We were on our way to the Slough
Revival Meetings in Lancaster when she stopped in front
of the lion in Reservoir Park," recalls Alice Hershey,
who posed behind the wheel.

Ruth took a few steps backward, driving-wise, when she
married Willis Hershey. Willis had a horse and
carriage, instead of a car.

Friends on a Sunday afternoon outing. Ruth saw the
unusual visual possibilities in this roadside angle and
hairpin curve.

A caravan in the village of Paradise. Despite their
dress clothes, this gathering in front of Ruth's Uncle
Aaron Hershey's house appears to be rescuing a
stalled car (notice the tether between the roadster
and the touring car).

Ruth Hershey was a contented woman. She maintained the trust of her faith community and family, yet "she wasn't afraid to try things," as her friend Alice Hershey says. "She enjoyed living very much. She wasn't on the fringe. She was a leader."

The farm was her home. But it never held her captive. Her magazines, her friendships, her music, her photography, and her intrigue with what lay beyond Paradise, held a balance within her. A chartered Conestoga Transportation Company bus, based in Lancaster, drew her admiration and interest—an index to the scope of this Mennonite farm woman's world.

Dorothy and Hulda both remember their mother's experiments with photographing lightning. "When we were children, she mounted her camera on a stool on the front porch so it wouldn't shake. Then she opened up the box for a time exposure—I'm sure she read about it somewhere—all the while exclaiming about how pretty it was. We children sat on the porch and watched—and we weren't afraid.

"She was always fascinated by eclipses. She would set her alarm so she could get up in the middle of the night to see it. I don't know if she ever photographed one or not, but I bet she tried."

How the Photos Were Found

When Ruth Hershey's possessions were divided among her children in 1978, her daughter Katherine claimed a humble-looking box, stuffed full of little envelopes containing photograph negatives. Katherine salvaged it for her son Ed Huddle, a professional photographer.

"The negatives weren't organized, and I didn't have an enlarger that could handle negatives that size, so I ignored them for several years," explains Ed. "Then last spring when I was preparing for a lecture about *my* work, I decided to see what my grandmother had done. I bought an appropriate enlarger and discovered what is collected here."

The moment revealed Ruth Hershey's artistry and created an emotional connection for her grandson. "Until then, her work had not been enlarged. Because of the limited equipment available to her, she made prints the same size as the negatives. I was suddenly able to understand Grandma Hershey with new eyes. I wasn't afraid of her as a child, but she was a little rough and gruff. She wasn't real warm, she wasn't overly organized, and she had a mind of her own! Now that I'm an adult, I'm beginning to understand her as a woman of accomplishment!"

Ruth Hershey's little box camera is now in Ed's possession, along with a wooden box marked "Kodak," which she likely used for mixing chemicals. No other pieces of her equipment have been found, and family members' memories of her developing process are incomplete. But partial information and Ed's professional hunch suggests the following.

Ruth bought chemicals at Darmstaetter's, a stationery store in downtown Lancaster. She developed the film into negatives in total darkness in a closet at home. It appears likely that she made prints by placing the negatives against daylight sensitive paper, then exposing it briefly to daylight.

The Sears and Roebuck catalogs published in the early 1900s carried photo-developing equipment, geared for home use. One could buy a "printing frame," which held the negative and paper together and which had a little door that one could swing open to expose the negative to light, ideally outdoor light. Some "Daylight" paper required no developer, but was used with fixer only.

In those days before electricity, the home darkroom enthusiast could also buy a kerosene lamp for use when developing film. Neither a lamp nor a printing frame has

Ed Huddle with some of his grandmother's
photography equipment.

been found among Ruth Hershey's equipment.

Ed has discovered evidence of his grandmother's frustration with the limitations of her camera. "A lot of her negatives show that she tried to photograph her subjects at close range. But the early box camera [the Kodak model was first available for home use in 1900] had a fixed lens. So she got roll upon roll of blurred shots. She obviously gave up trying after awhile, but that was a fairly expensive experiment in those days!"

What about the photographs in which she is present? Ed assumes she operated as he sometimes does. "I am sure she set up the shot, planning how she and the others would appear, then asked a bystander to push the button. The negatives are hers—so the angle, the composition, and the light were her work." Ruth Hershey the manager, the artist, the farm and family woman.

About the Photographer

Ruth Hershey Hershey, about whom this book is written, was born in 1895 east of Lancaster, Pennsylvania. She took photographs with a small box camera and developed the negatives and prints herself, without any training or intention of sharing her work beyond her family. Most of the photographs in this collection were taken between 1915 and 1940.

Ruth Hershey died in 1990, while a resident at the Mennonite Home, west of Lancaster.

Author

Phyllis Pellman Good, Lancaster, Pennsylvania, is a book editor and editor of *Festival Quarterly,* a magazine exploring the art, faith, and culture of Mennonite peoples. She is co-editor of the book *Perils of Professionalism,* co-writer with her husband, Merle, of *20 Most Asked Questions About the Amish and Mennonites,* as well as *Ideas for Families,* and author of several well-known cookbooks.

Together she and Merle are executive directors of The People's Place, The Old Country Store, and several associated galleries and museums in Intercourse, Pennsylvania.

Photography Editor and Printer

Edwin P. Huddle, who selected and printed the photographs in this collection, recently celebrated his twentieth year as a fine art photographer. Based in Lancaster, he works primarily in black-and-white photography, ranging in subjects from portraits to seascapes to Lancaster County countryside.

He is the grandson of Ruth Hershey, the son of her daughter Katherine.

"In the earliest decades of the twentieth century,
many young Mennonite women participated in girl crowds.
Ruth Hershey was among them."